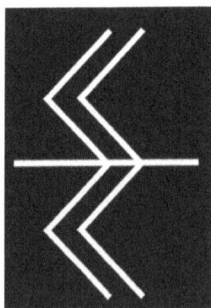

A Broken River Books original

Broken River Books
12205 Elkhorn Ct.
El Paso, TX 79936

ISBN: 978-1-940885-42-1

Printed in the USA.

THE
BROKEN RIVER
REVIEW

#1

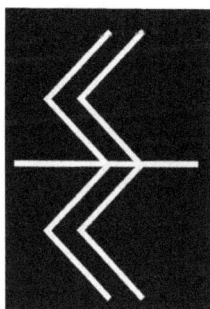

BROKEN RIVER BOOKS
EL PASO, TX

Thank you for picking up the first edition of *The Broken River Review*. For those of you unfamiliar with Broken River, we are a small press located in El Paso, TX specializing in "weird crime fiction."

For those of you familiar with Broken River Books: hey! How's it going?

Inside this magazine you'll find two pieces of fiction, and two pieces of non-fiction.

I like this formula. It's simple, quick, and fun.

I'm pleased with it, and I think you will be, too.

Thanks so much for your support.

With Love,

JDO
El Paso, TX
7/15/2018

THE TRANSCENDENTAL NUMBER

by
Nick Mamatas

The Olympic Diner didn't close during Hurricane Sandy, even when ankle-deep floodwaters entered and the servers had to splash from table to table, delivering French fries and Manhattan clam chowder. That's the red stuff, not the creamy New England soup. It didn't close on 9/11 either. In fact, it was packed all day. Customers crowded into booths and put four-tops together to discuss killing every Arab in the world, or the possibility of martial law, through mouthfuls of silver dollar pancakes and bacon-topped hamburgers. The Olympic hadn't closed since it opened, not for the New York City blackout in 1977, not when The Greek's children were born.

And The Greek, the day's newspapers spread before him, golf pencil in hand, doodled and figured all day, every day. When the diner opened, The Greek had been a svelte man with dark hair in thick waves, and teeth thick and white as dice. He smoked in his corner booth until the day the man from the city showed up with the No Smoking sign and made him grind out his last butt. The walls around the booth are still stained yellow. When The Greek's mother died, the Olympic Diner didn't close, but the back room was stuffed with family eating the *makaria*—the mercy meal of broiled fish—after her funeral. When the Greek died, he hoped his wife and children would eat the same meal, and step out to serve customers as best they could.

The Greek was old. He was bald save for a gray bundt cake of hair ringing the back of his head. His barrel chest collapsed, and his forearms were flabby. He still had the newspapers, but they comprised a sloppy tablecloth on which he rested his iPad. Now he typed, and occasionally played blackjack, on the machine as his son and daughter ran the place.

"Pop," Kalliope said to her father, loudly because The Greek was going deaf. "Pie?" She had a thin slice of berry pie on a plain white saucer. She was a good Greek girl, with a wide face and curls. Not so pretty that she caused a lot of problems; strong enough to bus tables of ten. This was how The Greek thought.

"Pee," The Greek said, looking up at his daughter. That was his joke, an old one. "Pie" is how Americas say π. But it's actually pronounced like the English letter p. He laughed and Kalliope laughed and he happily ate his pie.

Kalliope glanced down at the figures The Greek was working on. "Gee Pop, working on the bills or the ponies?"

"If I knew about the ponies, I wouldn't worry about the bills," The Greek said. Then he asked "What time it is?" in his foreign way. He rubbed his wrist, where he used to wear a watch.

"Right here—3:10," Kalliope said, pointing to the tiny digital readout on the right-hand side of the iPad's screen.

"Okay, good," he said, and without another word or even a smile for his daughter he collected his iPad and went into the kitchen, then through it, to the Olympic's tiny office. There he withdrew a revolver from his desk drawer and a box of ammunition, and carefully loaded every chamber in the cylinder. The Greek stuffed the revolver in his pants, not bothering to obscure it at all.

The Greek had a name. Archimedes Spanakos. He was not The Greek back when he was a child in Greece; he was just another Greek on an island full of them. Milking goats, shitting in an outhouse, crossing himself when he walked past the church on the way to school or when he rode past it on the back of his uncle's pick-up truck twice a year when delivering ripe olives to the docks for export to the mainland.

And school. The Greek was just another kid in that one-room schoolhouse, reciting poems and doing sums and learning about ancient Greek heroes and the villainous Turks. The Greek applied himself just enough to avoid his mother's *koutala*. She'd beat his ass with it, then go right back to stirring the evening soup with it.

Then one day, the teacher explained π. Not the letter— the seemingly impossible, utterly endless and unpredictable number. The teacher proposed a competition; whichever boy could recite the most digits of π would win a prize. The teacher had a book with several pages of numbers and the boys were allowed to copy from it, to bring the numbers home to memorize and recite. The Greek couldn't write down all the numbers, but he filled a piece of scratch paper with two pages of numbers and took them home.

The Greek took the contest seriously. He'd heard that, in America, phone numbers had seven digits because those were easy to memorize, so he broke his list of digits into groups of seven, and got to work. The teacher was right— there was no pattern to the numbers at all. The Greek got to 35 digits, including the 3 on the left side of the decimal, and then saw that the number after the 35th, an eight, was also an eight. Thirty-six digits. *That had to be enough*, he thought. The Greek imagined that he had a phone number, that his mother had one and that miraculously that his father had a separate phone number. Then he gave his small sister Argyro a phone number too, and just to be safe gave the fifth phone number to Jesus Christ. The final eight was easy to remember, plus it made sense. Seven is a lucky number, and eight is one more than seven so it must be *one more luckier*.

The Greek dominated the competition. The smartest boy in the class, the priest's son Constantine, memorized twelve digits. The second smartest boy, a scrawny crybaby named Vassilis stumbled early on, reciting *three four one* by accident.

π changed things. His teacher took The Greek seriously now, and the prize, a hardback edition of Homer's *Odyssey*, inspired The Greek to spend more time on his uncle's small fishing boat. The Greek was groomed to go to trade school, and then to the Navy where he grew strong in the engine room of the destroyer *Niki*, which was once an American ship. And there was always π. Reciting digits was a party trick, something to do while drunk. He learned dozens of digits, and pored over them on the long shifts aboard *Niki*.

Then, America. The colonels led their coup while The Greek was at sea, so the Greek walked off the ship one day and never returned. It took months of semi-legal work on the yachts of the wealthy, on fishing boats, and finally, on a big tanker, but he made it to the United States. To New York.

In America, people shortened the Greek's name to Archie. On the local boxing circuit he went by Popeye—a play on his last name, which means spinach. In America, money was like π; it went on without end. The Greek busted hump for a cousin's restaurant in Queens, saving his purses when he managed to knock out some *mavro*, and breaking thumbs for a bookmaker on the rare occasions when he had to.

This was all before he got married—married in the Greek Orthodox Church, where he and betrothed Elpida wore the *stefana* that bound their souls together. With the *prika* from his wife's father, he opened the Olympic diner. At the Olympic, he became simply The Greek in a neighborhood full of Italians, Chinese, Jews, Russians, and *mavro*. The Only Greek. Like a digit of π, seemingly floating without connection to any other.

Seemingly.

Even Elpida wasn't called anything but Mrs. Spanakos, though honestly she was more Greek than The Greek. The Greek liked American TV, got a kick out of the idea of the Easter Bunny, and loved carving turkeys on Thanksgiving right on the Olympic's lunch counter as family, friends and customers mixed together among the tables, but Elpida had never fully left the old country. When The Greek died, Elpida would surely snap off the radio one last time, and take up the black clothing of a widow. *But not today, God willing*, he thought as he walked back through the kitchen, but that thought was just a reflex. The line crew all had their heads low and bent over half-made salads or the deep fryer or the long sizzling grill, so they didn't see The Greek's gun.

You see, The Greek had discovered something about π unknown to all the scientists and mathematicians of the world, and all the priests and monks as well. An infinite number of numerals meant that everything was contained in π. Somewhere, Archimedes Spanakos was there, as was the olive pit on which he had chipped a tooth at age four. Jesus Christ was in there, as was Adolf Hitler, and Homer, and even the Olympic Diner at 3:14pm one afternoon in June.

One just needed to turn the numbers to letters somehow.

Ten digits, twenty-four Greek letters, but once upon a time Greeks had used their alphabet, specially marked, for numerals. The Greek had learned the system as a boy.

A′ for 1.

B′ for 2.

Γ′ for 3.

Δ′ for 4.

Apha, beta, gamma, delta, and so on.

Even π meant something other than 3.14... in the old system.

With the little mark next to it, π meant 80.

That was what made deciphering the infinite chant of π so complex.

Did 3.14 equal **ΓAΔ**—three, one, and four?
Did 3.14 equal **ΓIΔ**—three, and fourteen?

Did 3.14 equal ΛAΔ —thirty-one, and four?
Did 3.14 equal TIΔ—three hundred and fourteen?

And so on.

If the numbers didn't translate into sensible Greek one way, he tried combining numbers into tens, hundreds, or thouands until he got comprehensible sentences.

Sentences that predicted the future. Sentences from outside of time. Sentences from God, who lives outside of time.

When he was a boy The Greek had prayed for the soul of his dead *papou*, a brigand and a killer. Not because his mama had commanded him to with the threat of the koutala, and not because God would ever bring a soul from hell into heaven, but because God already knew that a little Greek boy would pray for his dead grandfather and had counted it in papou's favor before the prayer had even been said. The Greek had to have said the prayer, as God had already counted it. And so he had prayed.

π worked the same way.

The Greek had learned of the moment about to unfold years ago, and hoped that the prayers his children would say for him tomorrow would count for something.

His son Kostas, who was wiping down the counter, spotted The Greek coming out to the front of the house, and then saw the gun.

"Pop..." he started, then he followed the Greek's eyes. The bell tied to the Olympic's front door rang and three men entered. Kalliope picked three thick, glossy menus from the lunch counter and moved to greet them, but The Greek stepped in front of her. He glanced at the clock atop

16

the door, and the time was right. 3:14. One of the men reached to turn the sign hanging from the door so that the side reading SORRY, WE'RE CLOSED faced out. These were the men predicted by π. *Mafiosi*. Brigands and killers, looking for protection money, ready to burn down the Olympic Diner, rape the Greek's daughter, kill his son. Elpida would drown in tears.

The Greek drew his revolver and shot the first man. Kalliope screamed. The second man pulled out a gun of his own, but The Greek was faster and shot him too.

Then The Greek couldn't feel his left arm. He thought he heard angels coming for him, but it might have been the clatter of spilling flatware, or a bullet shattering glass. The third man stood over him, with a gun much larger than The Greek's.

Kostas handed Kalliope a pot of hot coffee and Kalliope flung its contents in the third man's face. He clawed at his skin, howling.

The Greek, on his back, something slick and wet like spilled syrup under him, lifted his revolver, and prayed. *Γιος του πατέρα άγιο πνεύμα.*

Son, and a bullet in the man's belly.

The father, and another bullet, this one in the man's chest.

The Holy Spirit, and the man's forehead opened up and out fell his brains.

The Greek looked up and saw his children staring down at him. He wanted to recite π to them, to explain that everything would be all right. They could close the Olympic, take the life insurance money, go somewhere and be real Americans. Marry *xeni* and allow their spouses to name his grandchildren Kaylee and Aiden and Josh, celebrate Easter when the Western calendar said they should. The grandkids wouldn't even have to pray for their poor dead papou, because everything was already settled.

But The Greek knew that wasn't so. He put the revolver on the floor and picked it up again by the hot barrel, and handed it to Kostas.

"Get more bullets," was the last thing The Greek said. "You're going to need them."

LOVE LETTERS

by
Steve Rasnic Tem

So two years after we split up I went back across the country to retrieve every message she wrote, just to remind her how she used to feel about me. It would be a pretty big deal if I could pull that off—what female wouldn't be knocked off her heels by something like that?

Sometimes people tried to stop me from retrieving those messages and I had to hurt them. It's unfortunate—I don't like to be violent, but sometimes violence occurs when you're committed to a goal. Also when you're in love.

I know—not every note Karen wrote had my name written down like in a letter (although some of them surely did), but they were still intended for me. I was with her when she wrote them, and we were in love, at least I thought we were, and we had an understanding, at least I did.

It was just one of those crazy summers, I guess. We met in this used bookstore in San Francisco, and I told her how much I liked that Hunter Thompson guy, and I talked about how he and I had both lived in the same town in Colorado for a while. She looked at me like I was almost famous. I guess I let her think I knew him better than I did, but I was so impressed with her—I just couldn't stop looking at her. When I said I was thinking about hitchhiking around the country I couldn't believe she wanted to go with me.

I had just been bullshitting with her. I came up with that hitchhiking idea just so she would stay and talk with me a little longer. But before I knew it we had a plan, and then we were on our way.

I drove a van that second time when I went back for her love letters. It would have taken forever to hitchhike (as it was it took me nearly five years). First I had to find them all, and then I had to figure out how to get them—because she'd written on all kinds of things, some of them pretty big. I was ready for anything, even a little jail time if I was caught. I wanted to do this right. I wanted to do it like a legend.

Outside Salinas, Kansas she'd written me a note on the side of a soda pop machine. It was an old one, a collector's item I guess if it were in better shape. It was rusty and empty and the red paint had faded pink. Back when she wrote the note it had still been working. I'd even bought us a couple of sodas out of it. She wrote: "Dear Frank, If I had known you years ago and we had lived here you could have bought me a Coke and we could have sat out here watching the cars go by to better places we could only imagine because this was the only place we had ever known. XXX, Karen."

She was dreamy like that, like anything was possible if you didn't think too hard about it.

I don't know what kind of marker she'd used—she carried a rainbow of a beaded bag that was full of all kinds of pens and paints and markers and a journal too. But it must have been a good one because the message was still there two years later with a halo around it where the paint had faded. I guess it was some kind of reaction with the paint and the sun—who knows—it was like magic and I didn't want to figure past that.

I dragged a low bench against the front of it for leverage, and then I backed the van up and manned it in with my shoulders and hands. Good thing it was empty and not as heavy as the new ones. Then I got a job for a couple of weeks sweeping parking lots while I figured out how to get my letter cut out. I bought a drill and a grinding wheel out of my wages and a few hours later I had my letter and I dumped the old machine in a ditch and I was on my way again, feeling like a hero.

It's hard to describe how much I appreciated the things she wrote. It was like reading a favorite writer. You're excited every time something new comes out—it feels like that writer understands you and speaks only to you. And even when a book doesn't seem to have anything to do with you, you figure the writer just made a mistake, and the next one will make up for it. Sometimes they do and sometimes they don't, and when they don't it can be pretty upsetting.

I remembered "Somehow I found," but it turned out to be "Someday I'll find" scratched into that metal Parking for Customers ONLY sign in downtown St. Louis. "Someday I'll find the right guy for me and I'll settle down with some kids and a nice house. That's not happening now but it WILL happen." I'd been inside the store shoplifting some food so when I ran out and saw her scratching away I only had time for a quick read and a grin before we ran down the alley.

I admit I was disappointed when I read it the second time but I decided to take it anyway, crowbarred the whole thing off the wall and stuck it in the van. Ran a fellow over peeling out of the lot. I couldn't stop and he shouldn't have been there. I figure he was either a guard or a homeless guy, so either way he knew the risks.

I would have asked her to marry me back then if I'd thought she'd say yes. But she wasn't too serious about anything and asking her would have ruined whatever it was. But even then I wanted to find something that would last, even if later on I wished it hadn't, if that makes any sense.

Sometimes we'd camp on the edge of a town in a little patch of woods or by a stream, and she'd look up at the stars and say things like "did you ever" or "can you imagine" and sometimes she'd stand up and do a little dance and laugh, her mop of curly red hair shaking like it was electrified. I didn't exactly feel any of the things she was saying, but I was really glad that she did.

We actually didn't have sex that often, definitely not as often as I wanted to, but she was always so nervous and high strung I figured she just didn't want to take the time. I always figured there would be more opportunities for that later on.

I remembered we stayed over a week camping out by a lake somewhere in southern Wisconsin. Karen had wandered all over the woods, and when she found a tree she especially liked she'd scratch a word or three into the bark. "Wonderful" and "true to itself" and "someday a house?" and "sturdy" and stuff like that. Each message was nothing special by itself, but she said those woods were like her "living poem. See, Frank—it's the accumulation and the sum total of all these words around us, warping and changing as these trees get bigger and older." I wasn't so sure I got what she was saying, but she sure was in love with the idea.

The problem was I had no idea which lake it had been, which shore, which anything, so I drove around that part of the state for weeks looking for something that looked familiar, except we had been there in mid-summer and now it was the fall and everything was different and damn cold in the evenings. But again—proof positive this whole adventure was blessed—I found this fence by a gravel road one day and I knew positively I'd seen it before and after a day of looking on both sides of that lake I found the very spot where we had camped and that first tree—"harmless," carved out in these funky straight lines and sharp angles.

I wasn't sure how I was going to get those words out, mind you, but I'd brought along a chainsaw full of gas and some axes and knives and even a bunch of rolls of duct tape and tubes of glue with this very job in mind.

I didn't know if anybody was going to give me any trouble over what I was going to do. I didn't much care, but I didn't see any houses around so I went right to finding the trees with writing on them and cutting the thinner ones down so I could cut the whole section out. The only thing to do with the ones too thick for the saw was to take a section of the bark off under the message as carefully as I could, reinforcing the back with duct tape and gluing on any bits that fell off.

I may have gotten a little carried away on those thinner trees. I really didn't know how many trees she'd put messages on—but I knew it was a lot—and sometimes I found these squiggly lines in the bark that might have been letters that had mutated because of growth or weather—I couldn't be sure—so I cut those down to study later, just in case. But after awhile there were trees leaning against trees and hiding other trees and it all got a little confusing. And she and I had wandered all over those woods, sometimes together and sometimes apart. This second time—well, I was there for months. Nobody cared, nobody came by. I got a part-time job at a garage in town—not much money, but enough for food and extra blankets. The place began to feel like home.

Then one day I felt like a steak, but I didn't have any money. So I shoplifted it at the local Walmart, which has everything anybody ever needed to be happy I guess. I got back into the van with it, then realized I didn't have anything with which to cook the steak on my campfire, so I went back into Walmart and shoplifted a frying pan. They grabbed me on the way out.

It was just a fucking frying pan. Problem was I explained what I had done to the judge using those exact same words. She gave me six months in the county lock-up. At least my boss at the garage agreed to hold on to my van in his back lot.

I always planned to go back to the woods and finish the job when I got out. But while I was inside the story broke about the "senseless vandalism" that had occurred on a section of the local state forest land. There were "increased patrols" and "heightened security" for starters. So when they released me I picked up my van and left before I was quite done. So it would have to be an unfinished poem—but I figured there was something kind of sweet in the idea of that, so I let it go.

In Chicago, Karen and I spent a lot of time in one of the local libraries. She'd write things in some of the books. She said she felt guilty about it. I told her she couldn't help

27

herself—she had "a compulsion." People can't help having a condition. I was always trying to make her feel better.

At least I remembered that she'd only written in the novels, writing new and crazier, or happier endings for them, using her and my names for new characters. We'd show up at the last minute in the last chapter and change everything. So after a few weeks of examining everything in the fiction section and writing down the affected titles, I brought in a big box, packed everything up, grabbed a dolly I saw one of the workers pull out of a closet, and wheeled it out the front door. It seemed like the easiest way. If they stopped me I'd just tell them I was "moving these to the main branch." I mean—who would believe somebody could be so audacious? And they were just library books, so what was the big deal? I hadn't killed anybody—not there, not that day.

The alarm was a lot louder than I'd expected. That probably made that oh-so-confident look I'd practiced slip just a bit. But I just kept walking, right out the door and down the sidewalk at a pretty good clip. About a block away the guard caught up to me. That surprised me. I mean, when did they start putting guards in libraries? Maybe I just never noticed. It's kind of sad, really, when you think about it.

He was a really old guy in a blue shirt, like that blue shirt was supposed to give him some authority. He didn't even wear a badge, just the library's name with the symbol of a book sewn above his pocket. "Wait! Wait!" He was gasping. I don't think he was used to running. "Could I just get your . . ." He was too out of breath to talk anymore, but his legs were still moving, getting him closer to me.

I stopped then, he was so polite. I looked at him. He was older than my dad. He didn't wear a gun, but he had this little black spray bottle in a holster on his belt. I figured it was mace, or maybe just pepper spray. Yeah, pepper spray. I shoved him so that he went down hard backwards over this little retaining wall. I mean hard. I don't think he even moved after that. I walked on down the street with the books to my van around the corner.

I travelled all over the place. Kentucky, Tennessee, down to New Orleans, over to New Mexico. I even went to places we probably hadn't visited during our hitchhiking, but I wanted to be sure, and my memory gets mixed up

29

sometimes, so if I remembered we'd talked about going to a place, or even just wanted to go to a place, or if I had been somewhere before but couldn't remember the exact circumstances, I added it to the itinerary. Five years, or almost. I arrived back in town with the van mostly full of signs and tree parts and books and metal bits and sections of picnic tables and hunks of concrete and some stolen art and an old tire from a field that had my name on it and somebody's firewood box and a few pieces of wallboard and some wallpaper and a lot of random trash I had no memory of collecting.

Some folks tried to stop me and paid a price that was non-proportional. I couldn't remember them all—I tried to pay attention only to myself and what I needed to do.

She wasn't happy to see me. I mean, she *really* wasn't happy when I pulled up in that trashed-out van to her new life looking pretty much the same as I had years before. And I have to admit I was a little surprised to see her. Because she *had* changed—a little more weight (which did look good on her), and her hair wasn't bright red and curly anymore.

It was brown and pretty much straight. And she had two little kids, standing just inside the door, and a husband as well, standing behind them, and looking suspicious.

"It's okay, Reggie—I got this," tossed back over her shoulder like she was in charge. Hell, she *was* in charge—that was the biggest change. She walked down the sidewalk to my van so fast I had no choice but to follow.

"Frank! What are you *doing* here?"

I looked at her, trying to feel angry about the way she said it, but not quite able to. "I went back," I said, "to all those places we visited that summer. I brought your love ... I brought your letters back."

"Letters? What are you talking about?"

That's when I opened the back door of the van like it was some kind of showcase, and I swept my arm around like a magician at the end of his last trick. I don't think she had any idea what she was looking at, at first, then after a minute or two she turned and stared at me.

"You scare me, Frank," she said, not sounding mad at all. And not really sounding scared, either. Sad, I guess. She

sounded sad. "And you know something? You always did."
She walked back up the sidewalk and into her house.

That's when I realized that while I'd been crazy back then, she'd just been young and playing a part.

It took me awhile to find a safe place to dump all her letters, everything I thought I knew about her, someplace where I didn't think I'd get caught. I even dumped the tools—I just didn't want them anymore.

Sometimes something changes so much it's like the thing you loved has died. So you either stay there with the body or you move on.

But still, I didn't get mad. And that really surprised me. Actually I was kind of grateful. Adding up the part of a year we spent hitchhiking, and the over two years I spent thinking about her, and the close to five years I spent hunting and collecting and getting that stuff right to her door—that was eight whole years of my life I'd managed to fill. Now I just had to figure out what to do with whatever time I had left.

COPS

by
Benjamin Whitmer

If you're surprised that cops get away with murder, you're soft on your history. If you're surprised people are pissed off about it, you're soft on your ethics.

That's the first line I wrote for an article I proposed to J David Osborne just after riots broke out in Ferguson Missouri, when a grand jury decided not to indict killer cop Darren Wilson for murdering the unarmed teenager Michael Brown. The article was postponed, but as I told Osborne, I had no doubt there'd be another cop killing when he was ready for it.

See, I'm old enough that there's no excuse for my being soft on this history. I remember the not guilty verdict for the four cops that lead to the 1992 Los Angeles uprising. And I lived in Cincinnati shortly after the riots in 2001, resulting from another killer cop who was ultimately acquitted. More, I remember watching the Cincinnati police kill person after person without consequence in the years after. The ugliest was one black man who was choked to death outside of a White Tower for dancing.

I've also been lucky enough to live much of my adult life in Denver, where the last time anyone looked, 2010, the city ranked number one in the nation in excessive force complaints, with no consequences whatsoever visited upon a single officer that I can recall. Something that came as no surprise to anyone who lived here, given the epidemic of cop killings.

So I am never surprised when cops murder, nor when they get away with it. At my age, to be surprised would be a kind of willful ignorance bordering on insanity. Even in the most notorious police scandal of my lifetime, the Rampart CRASH unit scandal, which hinged in large part on the cover-up of multiple unprovoked murders, not a single officer served a day in prison.

That is not to say that no cop has ever been held accountable for his or her actions. Justin Volpe, for instance, is doing 30 years for sodomizing Abner Louima with a broken broomstick in a New York precinct bathroom. But, of course, the officer who helped him hasn't served a day, nor the four other officers who helped cover it up.

Cops just aren't held to the same standards as the rest of us. I've spent a lifetime learning that lesson. And the people who pay the cost are the poor, the mentally ill, and people of color, with American Indians far and away the racial group most likely to be killed.

It's also something I've become personally acquainted with. I just returned from my small hometown in Southern Ohio, population 3,000, where family and friends placed a memorial plaque on a dogwood tree planted for one of my best friends, Paul Schenk, who was murdered by the police two years ago.

* * *

Paul'd had a bad day. His cat had died, he'd had a disagreement with his son, and he was in chronic pain. He'd been drinking too much, and when the police came to investigate a disturbance, he was in a state where it was easy to provoke him. So they did. And within an hour, he was trapped in his apartment, surrounded by armored vehicles, a helicopter, and nearly 100 SWAT members and local police officers.

While his friends and family, including his thirteen-year-old daughter, begged for a chance to talk him out, the police used the armored vehicles to provoke his fire, so that they could pinpoint his muzzle flash and get a good sight picture. When they did, one of the snipers shot him in the head. His last words were, "Y'all fuckers are trying to kill me."

And they were. Major Kirk Keller of the Greene County Regional SWAT made that clear in an interview afterwards.

They never had any intention of negotiating with Paul; they came to kill him. That there was no reason to kill him was irrelevant. There were no hostages, nobody was in any danger that the police weren't causing, and Paul was in his own house. There was no reason to do anything but wait for him to come out. But they had a chance to kill him, knew there would be no consequences, and they did.

To be clear, Paul was not unarmed. He fired nearly 200 rounds during the standoff, though never hitting anyone. Most of the shots were into his own roof or walls in an attempt to keep the cops back. He wasn't soft on his history. He'd been around long enough to know they were there to kill him. I don't have a problem in the world with that. They picked the fight with him on his own property and did everything they could to escalate it. They came on like a military force. To my mind, that's exactly why the Second Amendment exists. The only problem I have with Paul's actions is that his aim wasn't better.

* * *

If that last line makes me sound a little bitter or angry, well, I am.

I'm furious. Every day.

See, it brings me to my second sentence about Ferguson: "If you're surprised people are pissed off about it, you're soft on your ethics." Because the only thing more sure than the lack of accountability for cops, is that when people get pissed off about it, lots of well-meaning folks will start tsk-tsking about "violence."

Maybe it's just me, but I'm a words guy. Meaning, I like using 'em for what they mean. So in the shooting of Michael Brown, I'd point out that shooting an unarmed teenager 12 times is indeed violent. But turning over a car or smashing a window, even setting a building on fire, is vandalism. Those are not the same thing. If you doubt that, I'd recommending striking a friend over the head with a tire iron and then doing the same to a window. Take careful note of the difference in pain levels evidenced by each.

People get pissed off because we have the right to be. And, if you want the truth, people getting pissed off is the only chance we have to make the cops stop killing people. It sure as hell won't come any other way.

Remember how I said that I was in Cincinnati shortly after the 2001 riots that were incited by the killing of an unarmed black man? Well, that situation was recently nearly repeated when Samuel Dubose was killed by University of Cincinnati police officer Raymond Tensing. It took no time before Tensing was indicted by Hamilton County prosecutor Joe Deters. And not only indicted, indicted for murder, with a life sentence as a possible outcome.

That is not something I've seen up until the last year: cops getting indicted for murder. Not to say it has never happened, but never to this degree. Ohio governor (and Republican presidential candidate) John Kasich has even signed an executive order that holds police to an "imminent threat" requirement in use of deadly force, much like the requirement that concealed carry permit holding civilians are held to. At least in theory, cops now have to obey the same law as the rest of us.

As they should. Police apologists like to trot out the danger of their occupation as an excuse for their murders, but last I checked, their job is not as dangerous as, say, that of loggers, commercial fishermen, sanitation engineers, roofers, construction workers, farmers, truck drivers, and miners. I've worked a number of those jobs, and I have managed to never shoot anybody while doing it.

To my mind, this movement towards police accountability is a direct outgrowth of the uprisings in Ferguson and elsewhere. As well as the work of the Black Lives Matter and Native Lives Matter movements, CopWatch, and the many other community activists who recognize this as the civil rights issue of our era. They're my heroes.

And anyone who disputes that is soft on their history. And ethics.

Approaching the Page

by
James Sallis

Summers I'd spend whole afternoons on the porch and still be there in the evening when locust and cicada began calling, filling the yard, that blurred green universe, with their strumming cries. I'd drag out an old white rocker, stack my books on the floor alongside. It was a screen porch, and the best times were when it rained.

The books were likely to be a strange lot. Biographies of Houdini and Robert-Houdin and Chung Ling Soo, cheap editions of science fiction novels liberated from my brother's shelves, books on Shelley or Oscar Wilde, a copy of *The Magazine of Fantasy & Science Fiction* with a new story by Fritz Leiber, an issue of *Fantastic Universe* devoted to Stanley Weinbaum, astronomy and mineralogy texts, the Johnson Smith & Co. novelty catalog, a book promising to teach you to speak twelve languages including Esperanto. At the time I gave little thought to what I might be seeking in those books, just knew there was something in there I needed, something I had to have. When years later, in college, I encountered stories of specific hunger, women peeling wallpaper off the walls and eating it because it had nutrients they needed, I understood.

Across the street stretched an acre or so of close-set shacks, tarpaper and plywood mostly. Thousands of black folk lived there, and all my playmates. Helena had a tire factory, a chemical plant, the river itself: it drew people from all over. Struggling many years later with my first guitar, I'd learn that Robert Johnson had lived a mile or so down the road. Other Delta bluesmen, Johnny Shines, Muddy Waters, Roosevelt Sykes, passed through, on their way up to Memphis, perhaps, stopping off to play at The Blue Moon half a block down from Nick's Café, or over radio station KFFA. Sonny Boy Williamson records still were played on KFFA every day at noon, The King Biscuit Hour. As a young man my father had worked as a policeman. He told me how Sonny Boy's band would turn up on the road crew most Mondays. Sonny Boy'd gone off to London and been revered there, recorded with the Yardbirds. Came back home with a checkered suit and bowler hat and all these stories no one believed.

Meanwhile, from the drive-in restaurant clinging like a boat dock to the edge of my grandfather's property flowed a continuous current of music, Hank Williams and Hank Snow, Arthur Alexander, lots of Jimmy Reed, often in pitched battle with the Mozart, Shostakovich and Mahler on my turntable. Other kids hummed Brian Hyland songs. I hummed Mozart horn concerti, nurturing the apartness that, even then, moved me towards being a writer.

My brother, now a philosopher, had gone to school with Harold Jenkins, later known as Conway Twitty. In one early poem, in London, I'd write:

My brother John, round
face at the edge of my bed, collaborations
of parental persuasion. Now a man too,
like the bowl of a pipe. A philosopher,
teacher; wife and two daughters
in far-off Pittsburgh.

Everything seemed to be about edges then. And everything, the entire wandering, ancient, ever-new world, seemed far-off. With books and voluminous correspondence, much as my father manipulated his duck call, hand opening and closing about the end the way my own, years later, would cup harmonicas, I brought that world in closer. I wrote to the editors of science fiction and magic magazines, to Willy Ley, to fellow teenagers taken with conjuring. One of my favorite correspondents attended military school and had, stored away in his garage at home, a complete stage illusion once the property of Howard Thurston. The local newspaper published my short stories whenever I sent them in. For a short time I served as editor of *Zombie*, a magic magazine published by and for teenagers, on the cover of which my geekish school picture appeared.

Almost a decade after, taking up again the habit of correspondence, I'd turn out reams of letters as I sat looking across Iowa cornfields listening to Sonny Boy Williamson, Paul Butterfield, Dylan. Some of these letters ran to twenty or thirty pages. It was in them that I taught myself to write.

And it was there, RFD 3, that I sold my first stories, three of them all at once in a matter of weeks.

For months, neglecting classes in Modern British Novel and French 201, I had sat in the student union rereading Sturgeon, everything I could find, and writing in longhand these absolutely awful stories, leading to a suspicion I'd later pass along to students: that each of us seems to have a certain amount of garbage aboard, a quota of words we must write out before the good stuff starts coming.

Suddenly, it did start. Walking down the street one day I was startled by a man stepping from a doorway. I hurried along to the student union, sat, and began: *Walking down the street on my way to see the Leech....* I put down Rilke's *Letter to a Young Poet* halfread to write my own futuristic version. I took the unspoken anger and ever-mounting resentment between my wife and self and forged them into a 6000-word psalm to silence, isolation and withdrawal: "A Few Last Words." The epigraph was from W.S. Merwin:

> *What is the silence*
> *a. As though it had a right to more*

The first few good poems came in a scatter then, too, but *that* great unfolding still lay ahead, in London, in a bedsitting room just off Portobello Road where often I'd write two or three poems a day and obsessively rewrite others -- as with the letters, teaching myself.

But it worked. I'd sneaked into literature through the back door, still the way I prefer to come and go.

The first books I read were science fiction and belonged to my brother, book club editions he'd bought for a dollar. *Puppet Masters*, which laid wide tire tracks across my imagination. Jerry Sohl's *Costigan's Needle*, various Van Vogts, Simak's *Ring Around the Sun* and *Mission of Gravity*, Bester's *The Demolished Man*. At the local library I had exhausted the children's section and, with my brother as spokesman, challenged the librarian, reading for her from a book taken at random off the shelf and receiving my adult card. Somewhere or another, probably on a visit to Memphis, I came across an issue of a magazine dedicated to Stanley Weinbaum which I read over and over, especially the biographical essay, and a British magazine titled *Nebula*, which listed the twenty top science fiction novels, books I'd for the most part never heard of, like George R. Stewart's *Earth Abides*, *Tiger! Tiger!* and *Children of the Atom*. Soon enough I'd searched them down and read them all.

The taste for details of writers' lives by this time had taken hold; I was reading huge books on Shelley, Wilde, Poe, Thomas Wolfe. On a drugstore rack I came across James Ramsey Ullman's novel about Rimbaud, *Day on Fire*. This was the beginning of my fascination with French literature, an interest soon bolstered with a mass-market paperback of Baudelaire translations by Edna St. Vincent Millay and George Dillon, an anthology of French poetry, I think from Random House, containing translations by Merwin among others, and, finally, by Francis Steegmuller's Apollinaire biography. Not surprising that Rimbaud, the eternal adolescent, should become the first French poet with whom I, adolescent myself, should fall in love. Apollinaire became the second, engendering ideals of lyricism and poetic freedom that began to shape my own shabby work. He was also the first poet I translated.

And now the cook's plucking geese.
Ah, fall of snow
falling, no
girl for my arms.

Third, and perhaps the most influential of all, was Blaise Cendrars, in whose *Prose du transsibérien et de la petite Jeanne de France* I locate the beginning and very fount of modern poetry. Of all the world's poems, it is this one -- this inexhaustible poem defining both our era and the poet's responsibility as witness -- that speaks to me most directly.

Et j'étais déjà si mauvais poète
Que je ne savais pas aller jusqu'au bout

Powerful magic had found its way to me. I was like a child fed sweets for the first time, a primitive shaman given scalpels and bone saws. *Why hadn't anyone told me?* I was dangerous.

But I wasn't, of course.

I was only another writer, just another who found intolerable the notion there wasn't something *more*. Like a truffle-hunting pig, I kept digging beneath. Beneath the gray of diurnal life, repetitive labor, the sucking mud of politics, stuccoed walls, tile floors and newspapers, TV newscasts.

Camus' invincible summer was under there somewhere. I'd find it.

Nick Mamatas is the author of several novels, including *I Am Providence* and *Hexen Sabbath*. His short fiction has appeared in *Best American Mystery Stories, Tiny Crimes,* and *Vancouver Noir* among other venues, and was recently collected in *The People's Republic of Everything*.

Steve Rasnic Tem is a past winner of the Bram Stoker, World Fantasy, and British Fantasy Awards. He has published over 430 short stories. The best of these are in *Figures Unseen: Selected Stories,* from Valancourt Books.

Benjamin Whitmer is the author of *Pike, Cry Father,* and *Satan is Real*, which he co-authored with Charlie Louvin.

Jim's 18th novel, *Sarah Jane,* is now with his agent. Next year sees a fifth poetry collection and a new edition of *Difficult Lives* ridden piggyback by an equal measure of essays and introductions, *Hitching Rides.*

For more information on Broken River Books, visit:

www.brokenriverbooks.com

or find me on Twitter:

@brbjdo

Thanks again for picking up the first *Broken River Review*.

I hope your day is going swell.

www.ingramcontent.com/pod-product-compliance
Lightning Source LLC
Chambersburg PA
CBHW021337290326
41933CB00038B/961